The Poetry Project: Job

The Poetry Project, Volume 2

Angela Williams

Published by Angela Williams, 2023.

While every precaution has been taken in the preparation of this book, the publisher assumes no responsibility for errors or omissions, or for damages resulting from the use of the information contained herein.

THE POETRY PROJECT: JOB

First edition. October 11, 2023.

Copyright © 2023 Angela Williams.

ISBN: 979-8223702269

Written by Angela Williams.

Table of Contents

Dedication

I dedicate this, my second book, to Jesus Christ, my first Love. He radically saved my soul 16 years ago and He walks with me daily, transforming me in body, mind, and spirit. I am so grateful for the Helper He has given me, the Holy Spirit, Who has inspired every word I've spoken that I pray brings glory to the name of God on High.

I also dedicate this work to my earthly first love, my husband, Will, who has urged me for years to use the talent and giftings our Father has given me to write a book. He is such a faithful follower of Christ and God-fearing man...I am so blessed to be his co-laborer in the Kingdom! Thank you, Pookie, for always believing in me. I could do nothing apart from Jesus and you.

And I can't *not* mention the rest of my family who loves and supports me and fills my life with love and joy. To my parents and siblings, my three grown children and your spouses...y'all fill my life with so much happiness and I can't wait til you all come to Jesus so we can be a powerful family unit in the Kingdom of Christ and God!!

And probably most of all...to my growing little family of grandbabies...you each fill my soul with *more* purpose and meaning as one of the greatest titles I've ever been so blessed by God to hold...MAMAW!!!! I will faithfully and without reservation do everything in my power to lead you closer to the heart of the Father in all I do.

I also have a loving, supportive family of brothers and sisters in Christ who faithfully walk life's journey with me and co-labor in Christ's Kingdom together, in purpose and grace. I am so blessed and I thank each one of you!!

For every reader of this page and book: His heart is for each and every single one of you. YOU are the apple of His eye. I pray you meet Him soon through repentance and faith in His Son, Who truly makes life worth living. Now and forever. Amen.

The Accuser's Hand in the Life of a Blameless Man (Job 1-5):

There was once a man who stood out from the rest;
His name was Job, and God put him to the test.
The Bible calls him "blameless, a man of complete integrity."
He kept himself from evil and feared the Almighty.
He was very rich and had ten children,
It was his regular practice to intercede to God for them.
He feared that in their partying and pleasure,
Decisions may be made that could affect them forever.
His children might curse God in their hearts,
So he made prayers and offerings as a safeguard.
One day the members of the heavenly court
Came to present themselves to the Lord.
The Accuser, Satan, arrived on the scene with them,
And God asked this tempter where he had been.
His response was that he had been patrolling the earth,
Watching everything going on and God asked if he'd observed
That Job, His servant, was the finest man down here.
Satan retorted that it was only God's blessings that caused Job to fear.
He said if He took everything away,
Surely Job would curse Him to His face.
The Lord was so sure of Job's faithfulness,
He permitted the Accuser to bring about this test.
God said he could take everything but his life,
So Satan set to sifting and all Job's animals and children died.

The messengers kept coming to Job with these reports,
One after another, describing loss of every sort.
We get a peek behind the heavenly curtain,
And see another interaction between the Lord and Satan.
Again, God suggests to him His servant, Job.
Satan says if he makes him sick, that'll be the final blow;
He was certain this would cause Job to curse the Lord,
But of this man's integrity, God was most assured.
So the Accuser went back to work tearing Job down,
He covered his body in boils, and now no one but his wife was around.
All that he had left at the end of the day,
Was his unwavering faith in God and his wife that (for some reason) got
to stay.
She was a tool in the hand of the one accusing,
Telling Job to "curse God and die" - exactly what he was pursuing.
As Job was undone in this miserable state,
We wonder just how much one man can take.
But his response to all this loss and grief
In his brokenness and mourning was to sit at Jesus' feet.
His friends then came to bring comfort and consolation,
They sat with him a week in silence then began a conversation.
Job spoke first and cursed his very birth,
He asked why God even brought him to this earth.
We can only imagine how this man was feeling,
Righteous before God yet experiencing so much suffering.
It is human nature to wonder and to question,
And a lot of times we don't know why certain things happen.
Just like Job, we can begin to doubt
And try to understand the reason that these things come about.
Job's first friend that spoke in "God's defense"
Was sure there was some sin in Job's life that needed to be confessed.
Eliphaz did well by defending God's majesty,

But where he went wrong was in judging Job incorrectly.
He started by commending Job for how he'd encouraged others,
But then he turns to pointing the finger at his brother.
I wonder how often I am a miserable "encourager,"
Speaking my own thoughts and not the Truth of the Father.
This is a wonderful story about the struggles of a blameless man,
A heavenly interaction, and an inside look at our enemy's plans.
We see how he works among us and must have God's permission,
And how God comes to our aid and defends our lowly position.
There is so much for us to learn in the Book of Job
Although it's a tale of great loss, it ends in triumphant hope.
I'm not going to spoil the rest of it now, we will see in the days ahead
How God's plan stands supreme and true to His name, He resurrects all
that was dead.

Job's is Blamed in the Midst of His Pain (Job 6-9):

Job and his friends continue their exchange;
Eliphaz insists Job must be to blame.
He urges Job to present his case to God,
And even goes so far as to assume that he's a fraud.
He talks about schemers, the prideful, and the fool
Says he's studied life and Job should listen to his counsel.
He claims he knows the secret to Job's restoration,
That this is punishment for sin and he's in need of God's correction.
He tells him to repent and he'll bear fruit again,
That the Lord will give back all that He took from him.
Job spoke again in his own defense;
Telling them to fear God and show mercy because his pain was so intense.
He told them to stop assuming his guilt,
He stood on his integrity and accepted what God had willed.
Job cried out to the Lord and asked Him to kill him.
He just wanted all this misery to end.
Job said he didn't have the strength to endure,
With all that had been taken, he had nothing else to live for.
He told the men to tell him what they thought that he'd done wrong,
That he was willing to humble himself and repent all along.
He said he would keep quiet and have a teachable spirit,
If there was something they could point out, he would gladly hear it.
Then we see a change in this conversation,

Job turns to God in all his desperation.

He reminds the Almighty that his life is but a vapor,

He ponders on who we are and how we could have His favor.

In great distress, he says he must complain,

And proceeds to lament over all of his pain.

He asks God to go ahead and take his life,

He's so miserable that he can't even find rest at night.

He tells God he knows how He examines us every morning,

And brings tests upon our lives often and without warning.

He asks the Lord to forgive his sin,

And take away this heavy burden.

Bildad, the other friend, then gives his input.

He says that Job's children deserved this punishment.

And it was right that God had killed them,

Because they must have sinned against Him.

He told Job to pray and clean up his life,

To live with integrity and God would treat him right.

That "He would surely rise up and restore his happy home,"

And give him replacements for everything now gone.

He then accuses Job of having forgotten his Maker,

Even goes on to say the godless fade away as a vapor.

This "friend," too, puts the blame on Job;

And says the solution is to live honorably and that God would restore his hope.

Next, we see Job agree to the claims

That these men have made about God and His ways.

He tells them about God's attributes,

Says that without warning, He can make the mountains move.

He speaks about God's anger, His wisdom, and His miracles,

His justice and His mercy, then says He wounds him without cause.

Job questions, "Who am I, to try to answer or reason with God?"

He said he wasn't even sure if he did, that he would get a response.

He admitted that the Almighty is the One who is strong
And that He puts us in our place, where we rightfully belong.
He says even though he's innocent, his mouth would pronounce him guilty,
And despite the fact that he's blameless, His Maker would see him as filthy.
He insists that God will judge him harshly,
And bring severe punishment upon him sharply.
Job gets to the point he says, "What's the use of trying?
Cleaning myself up on the outside, but inside I am dying."
He then prays to God asking for a Way,
If there was only a Mediator to come and stand in his place.
He asks God to bridge the gap and take away his fear,
For Someone to take the punishment and allow us to draw near.
Job confessed he couldn't do it in his own strength,
But our mighty Savior, Jesus, went to this great length.
What Job couldn't see in the midst of his trial,
Is that God was already working to bring us a Messiah.
And this is exactly what Christ our Lord has done,
He is the go-between, the Restoration, and our forever happy home.

Job Grieves the Treatment He Receives (Job 10-13):

Job continues to plead his case,
Crying out to the Lord with his soul's complaints.
He asks the Lord to show him his sin,
He claims his innocence again and again.
Job says he doesn't understand God's rejection,
When he knows that He formed him since conception.
He speaks of how God knitted him in the womb,
And gave him life and love, but now has turned it all to gloom.
He says He took everything away,
And asked why God didn't send him straight to the grave.
He accuses the Lord of coming against him with His fist,
Says He's completely destroyed him and he had no strength to resist.
Job cries to the Almighty for comfort,
Says to leave him alone to return to the dirt.
He truly wants his life to end,
All this suffering is just too much to comprehend.
Next, the third friend begins his interaction,
He also accuses Job of committing some infraction.
Zophar says that God is just in His ways,
That Job is mocking Him and should be put to shame.
He does say some things that truly are correct,
Points out God is supremely wise and worthy of all respect.
He recognizes that the Lord is in control,
Of everything in heaven and on the earth below.

He tells Job to prepare his heart,
Get rid of his sin and set himself apart.
God would take away his pain and restore to him his hope,
And then he would find rest and peace for his soul.
Job bounces back with a rebuttal to him,
Says it's easy to point the finger at someone else's sin.
Finding a brother's fault is easier to do,
Than restoring him with encouragement and walking in his shoes.
Job says that even animals know the ways of the Lord,
That He holds understanding and wisdom, and His judgment is sure.
He has strength to build up and power to destroy,
To conquer mighty nations, to avert or to deploy.
He holds it all in the palm of his hand,
Whatever He sets forth in the sovereignty of His plan.
Job tells his friend that they are both equal,
He's no better than him, for we are all sinful people.
But he wants to speak directly to God,
All the arguments the friends have given him are flawed.
He claims that their defense has been crafted with lies,
If they would just be silent, they'd show themselves wise.
He says he is ready to plead his case,
And that God may kill him but that's a risk he's willing to take.
He has no other hope but to ask for God's protection,
He seems to be trying to humbly seek His correction.
Job asks God to remove His heavy hand,
Not to terrify him with His presence, in which no man can stand.
He asks the Lord to summon him and says he will comply,
To allow Job to speak to Him and then hear His reply.
He wants to have a conversation,
To talk to the Almighty about all these accusations.
Job asks the Lord not to turn him away in his misery,
He felt like He was treating him as if he were His enemy.

He continues to feel as if he's been abandoned,
He's lost all hope and only became more saddened.
He was in the company of these three men,
But they were miserable counselors and not good friends.
Job knows in his heart that he's not really alone,
And as this exchange continues, he'll go before the throne.
He didn't understand at this point in the story,
That everything God does, He does it for His glory.
We all have questions and at times we're left to wonder,
But we can trust our God as we meditate and ponder.
His thoughts are higher and His ways more perfect
Than anything we can hope or expect.
One day we may all understand,
The joy of eternity through the pain in His plan.
We won't reach Him without suffering
And looking more like Jesus our King.
This is the goal when we reach the finish line and receive our Prize,
Trading in our sorrows and shame as every tear is wiped from our eyes.

A Broken-Hearted Man Questions the Almighty's Plan (Job 14-16):

Job continues apprising God of mankind's condition-
How frail we are, how weak in our affliction.
He reminds his Maker that we are just clay,
In the Potter's hand and He has all the say.
He's already determined the length of our lives,
Set our course in motion; nothing takes Him by surprise.
He is the great Designer, He has a Master plan,
He watches over creation, all the work of His hands.
Job then tells the Lord that man's death is final,
That once we reach the grave, there will be no revival.
He says that if he just had some hope,
Of living again after death, he could cope.
With all the struggles he's now enduring,
He would find the release of death reassuring.
He wishes that God would seal away his sins,
Cover all his guilt and make him innocent.
He then accuses God of setting people up to fail,
Says He destroys our hope and overpowers us when we're frail.
Job believes the Lord is afflicting him with trouble,
That there can't be any other explanation for this struggle.
Eliphaz starts in on Job again,
Tells him that it's by his own mouth that he's condemned.
What he's proclaiming with all of his words
Shows that he has no fear of the Lord.

He calls his friend "nothing but a windbag, full of empty chatter,"
Claims his sins are speaking and this is the subject matter.
If he would just be quiet and stop his accusations,
God would comfort him and help him through these tribulations.
He tells Job to stop turning against God in ways that are evil,
That the angels in heaven can't even be trusted, much less sinful people.
He then goes on to describe what happens
To those without God who always lose the battle.
He says that their whole life is full of vanity,
Shaking their fists at the Almighty.
Living in fear, aimless, to be destroyed,
Everything removed from them and emptiness will be their reward.
That God gives their possessions, so He can take them away too;
They conceive trouble, give birth to evil, and deceit is all they produce.
Wicked people may appear to prosper,
But their time is only as long as the Lord allows them to endure.
This friend's rebuke is a heavy warning,
And Job again says how terrible they've been during all his mourning.
He tells them they are miserable comforters,
That if they were in his shoes, he would be their encourager.
He would try to take away their grief,
But they only add to his suffering with the words that they speak.
Job turns once more to God to cry out in despair,
He ultimately accuses the Almighty of being unfair.
He says that he was quietly minding his own business,
When God stepped in and turned him over to sinners.
He claims the Lord broke him into pieces,
Violently crushing him with death and diseases.
He says he now wears burlap to show that what is left
Is brokenness and sorrow, and heaven is his witness.
He pleads with these friends to show a little more care,
But then reassures everyone that he knows His Advocate is there.

The Mediator that he longs for and still inquires about,
He didn't understand the Gospel, but we all get it now.
Job simply knew that his burdens were too much to bear,
Praise be to Jesus that we can bring Him all our cares.
Lay them down at the foot of the cross,
All of our sorrows, sadness, and loss.
He intercedes between us and God the Father,
And offers salvation, forgiveness, and acceptance we're all after.
We can look back now on Job's life and see,
That God in all His goodness did offer a Way for him to be free.

Job's Woes Turn to Hope (Job 17-20):

We pick up here with Job's continued defense,
He's wrestling with God and none of this makes sense.
He says his spirit is crushed and he's ready to die,
That everyone mocks and rejects him and won't even look him in the eye.
He asks for God to come to his aid,
But then says it's His fault that Job's been betrayed.
He says again that he has no more reason for hoping,
That everything's been stripped away and his heart is utterly broken.
Upon this wounded soul, Bildad comes with more,
Heaping condemnation just as he did before.
He talks again of the wicked and uses many words;
He doesn't show any empathy, just wants his opinions heard.
This friend goes at it again and again,
Speaking of God's righteous judgment of sin.
Job understands this and sticks with his protest.
He says that God has captured him in His net.
That he is not guilty of any wrongdoing,
So there is nothing just about the penalty ensuing.
He tells him that their words have been a crushing blow,
To kick a man when he's down is the lowest one can go.
These men have done nothing but accuse Job of sin,
And show themselves prideful and self-righteous time and again.
Job is certain that God is causing all of this,
He keeps crying out to Him and asks where is the justice.
That there is no reason for all of his suffering,

Everyone has turned against him and he's lost everything.
Even his family has been taken or has left him,
His servants, his friends, and most painfully, his children.
He begs now to be shown some mercy,
Says he can't go on being treated as everyone's enemy.
Job wishes that his words would be written down,
He didn't know it but they were, so we have them now!
And today, we're in the middle of his story,
With the next words he speaks, He gives God all the glory.
He says, "As for me, I know my Redeemer lives,"
And with a change of heart, praises are what he gives.
In the midst of his pain and all this devastation,
He remembers the truth and makes this declaration;
One day, he knows, the Lord is coming back,
He announces that He'll stand upon the earth at last!
Job seems now to have changed his position,
Speaking with confidence of the resurrection!
He gets overwhelmed at the marvelous thought
Of rising in his body after death to see God!
He mentions to these friends that they should fear His judgment,
Saying they are the ones deserving of His punishment.
Then comes Zophar chiming back in,
Going on about the fate of the wicked and those living in sin.
He said it was his spirit prompting his reply,
And with all this talk of evil, Job's guilt is what's implied.
He says that all who live this way surely are deserving,
Of God's anger and wrath that He has been reserving.
He claims this is their inheritance, their faithful reward,
What they will rightfully receive for rejecting the Lord.
This may be true and we can all agree,
That we can't live in rebellion and expect to be set free.
Every man knows that one day he'll meet his Maker,

And give an account for all his earthly labor.
But may we not misrepresent Him;
It's His kindness that leads us to repent.
Yes there will be judgment and all will give an account,
We must come to Him in faith to receive our crown-
The crown of eternal life that's offered to all of us,
Through the sacrifice on the cross of our Savior, Jesus.
From eternity past, God has written the truth on our hearts,
It doesn't make Him happy to tell some to depart.
But in all His great wisdom and love,
He allows us free will and watches from above.
He's a heavenly Father to those who receive,
And as Job had faith in the Redeemer, we must each believe.
We have an advantage that Job didn't have,
We know the end of the story-that God gives everything back.
This is an ongoing test of his character and faith;
God works in our lives in the very same way.
He is always drawing and purifying those,
Who trust in His name and who He truly knows.
If you've never understood His master plan,
Come to Him today; He's holding out His hand.
He has such wonderful things in store,
Continue to stay with me and soon, you'll also be sure.

Seeking for True Justice for the Wicked Among Us (Job 21-23):

Job spoke again and told the men to listen,
He had an issue with the explanations that they'd given.
He told them that his complaint was not against people,
That God was the One allowing such evil.
He questions why wicked people prosper,
Growing in riches and becoming mothers and fathers.
Getting to see children and grandchildren,
All while living a life of rebellion.
That God doesn't punish them the way that He should,
And this isn't fair when they reject the One Who is good.
Job can't understand why God continues to bless them,
When they don't seek to know Him or even respect Him.
He says they don't come to the Almighty to pray,
They don't give Him thanks and they surely don't obey.
They believe that everything they have is their own,
And don't give God any glory for the prosperity they've known.
Job says again that none of this is fair,
Why does God show mercy to everyone, everywhere?
That we shouldn't all be treated as equals,
Some of us are good, but some of us are evil.
He believes that everyone should get what they deserve,
And that from the godless, His mercy ought to be reserved.
According to him, God's judgment must be brought swiftly and severely,
On all those who don't follow the Lord sincerely.

Not to punish their children, as his friends had claimed he would,
But to allow His anger to fall solely on the ones that it should.
He asks for every person living in sin,
To fall under God's wrath and experience destruction.
At this point in the conversation,
Job doesn't understand God's workings in all of creation.
He puts himself on the throne,
And claims to know better than the Almighty One.
How often do we make these same claims,
And think that we know best and God should do as *we* say?
Each of us ought to thank the Lord for His great mercy,
None of us are as righteous as we think we may be.
Outside of His grace and without His sacrifice,
Every one of us for our sin, would have to pay the price.
And this is a cost that none could afford,
But Jesus laid His life down that we could call Him Lord.
And this is what He deserves to be,
He takes our sins away and washes us clean.
This is the Good News that Job needed then,
God's grace over all mankind covering our sin.
We may not always understand His plan,
Drawing sinners to Himself and transforming them like only He can.
This is a beautiful thing that He does,
So let's not be so hasty to judge.
None of us deserve His infinite mercy,
But praise be to God that He considers us ALL worthy.
He can take the most unlikely character,
And transform them into a powerful messenger.
This, my friends, is the power of the Gospel,
I can't help but share it and when I do, it makes my heart swell.
But, let me get back to the men and their discussion,
Eliphaz comes back, blaming Job again.

He says that his friend is being self-righteous,
That God will judge him though, for his wickedness.
Remarks that there's no limit to the number of his sins,
His suffering is obviously due to him having cheated, lied, and stolen.
This friend then tells Job that he has walked in darkness,
Thinking he's been hidden and that God hasn't noticed.
Then he assures him the Almighty sees us all,
That nothing is hidden and his judgment will fall.
He says that the righteous will be happy when the wicked,
Are destroyed in the fire and all the earth is sifted.
Then he tells Job once more,
To submit to God and he would be restored.
To listen to the Lord and clean up his life,
To make the Almighty his joy and delight.
He said that if Job came to God to pray,
That God would accept him and set him on His way.
He would light up his path, hear him, and save,
But he must fulfill the vows that he's made.
He told Job he could then intercede,
And that God would set those sinners free.
Job speaks in response to all that Eliphaz said,
He knows if God would hear him, his case would be acquitted.
But he feels like He just cannot find Him,
Says he's searched in every direction.
He knows in his heart that He is still there,
And that if He examines him, He will be fair.
Job continues to maintain his innocence,
But says he is terrified at the thought of God's presence.
He knows that God is testing him,
And he will come out of all this in the end.
He has been examined and he will be tried,
But it's through the fire that we are purified.

Job's holding fast to the character of the Lord,
This is what we all must do - stand on His Word.
A lot of what these men are saying
Is true and we should each be weighing
The things that they've said about God and His nature,
Do we have a correct view of our Maker?
Do you think we really can understand,
The intricacies of the sovereign Lord's plan?
The best thing, I think, that we can do
Is to love Him and each other, however He calls us to.
Let Him be God and trust in His ways,
Knowing He will always be with us, come what may.

Life is But a Vapor, Then We Meet Our Maker (Job 24-28):

Job continues with probing questions,

He ponders on life and makes some observations.

He notices that the wicked have freedom

To live however their evil hearts lead them.

He says that the godly must wait on the Lord,

And that through trouble, they must patiently endure.

While the unrighteous go about their daily lives,

Working evil in all they do, yet somehow they thrive.

He says wicked people rebel against the light.

They do all sorts of mischievous things in the night.

Night or day, it's all the same.

They are constantly walking in a rebellious way.

He then proclaims that God does take note,

And one day, He will dash all their hopes.

That they may live in security now,

But in the end, every knee will bow.

Job is sure of God's power and might.

He is the giver and taker of life.

Now, we see Bildad speak again,

This time it's short and sweet, in God's defense.

He also speaks of the Lord's great power,

Says He brings peace in the heavens through His angelic warriors.

He says there is no human pure in God's sight,

That in all His glory, He shines infinitely bright.

And lights up the earth so we can all see,

The great contrast between us and the Almighty.

These statements are true - there is such a chasm

Between us and Him, and His goodness we can't fathom.

He made a Way to bridge this gap,

And set us free from our enemy's trap.

Job sarcastically says to his friend,

"What an example of wisdom and mercy you've been!"

He goes on to marvel of God in creation,

How He set the world on its foundation.

He separated the waters and sky,

Made the divide between day and night.

By His Spirit, He made everything,

In beauty and splendor and this is only the beginning.

The Almighty works in different ways displaying His great power,

From silence to a still small voice, to awesome roaring thunder.

Job then turns back to making his defense,

Says until he dies, he'll maintain his integrity and innocence.

His conscience is clear as long as he lives,

He knows that the Lord takes and He gives.

And he says it's God Who's taken away his rights,

Made his soul bitter with the darkness of night.

He reverts to discussing the fate of the wicked,

How they have no real hope when God's grace they've resisted.

Their time of prosperity is truly fleeting,

And from the One Who gave it they keep retreating.

Wandering aimlessly from the Giver of life,

Creator, Sustainer, the One Who paid their price.

It doesn't make any sense to Job,

How people can exist on this earth without hope.

He says they look high and low for wisdom,

But it's not found in this world or its systems.

That God alone is supremely wise,
And He searches the earth, seeing all with His eyes.
He is looking to see if anyone is faithful,
Has a fear of the Lord and forsakes evil.
For this is what makes a man wise, says the Lord,
And how do we grow in fear? By reading His Word.
This is how we learn Who He is,
And all that He's done and what He expects.
He invites us into His majestic plan,
And if we accept, He walks with us hand in hand.
We are almost at the end of Job's chatter,
But we will hear from the final friend on the matter.
And after that, the human voices stop,
And from the whirlwind, we'll hear from God.
I know this has been a lot of back and forth,
But stick it out with me to hear the heart of the Lord.
So much goodness in His correction,
Job's whole story will change direction.

Job's Final Defense of His Innocence (Job 29-31):

This is the last of the words Job spoke,

He reminisced on the days when he had so much hope.

He told these friends that God was with him,

That he experienced His friendship surrounded by his children.

He said the Almighty took good care of him,

When he was in his prime, they were such close friends.

God lit up his path and led him along the way,

His blessings were abundant and he received honor at the city gates.

He told about how young and old both showed him respect,

How people who came for his counsel were always refreshed.

That he was a man of honor and everyone knew it,

But now they all mock him and his reputation is ruined.

He said that in those former days,

He helped orphans and widows and received everyone's praise.

He provided for the homeless and any who needed help;

All who came were satisfied with his kingly counsel.

Everything he said was comforting and wise,

Even when he was silent, they found a smile in his eyes.

Job thought that he would live a good, long life,

Surrounded by his family on the day that he died.

But now it's all been stripped away,

His honor is gone and all that's left is shame.

He said that everyone now is against him,

Opposing him from every direction.

His life is full of sorrow and unending depression,
God has come against him with such great aggression,
He says He's thrown him into the dirt,
So he cries out to Him in the midst of all this hurt.
But God doesn't hear him or give any response,
Job can't understand the reason for His absence.
He claims that the Almighty has turned a blind eye,
That in His great power, He's sending him to die.
He continues to lament about his immense pain,
Says he cries out for help but no one comes to his aid.
He comes once again with his protest,
Asking God to weigh him on the scales of justice.
He's sure that he will be found pure,
He's lived with honor and integrity and of this he is sure.
He made a covenant with the Almighty on high,
Never to look at a young woman with lust in his eyes.
He speaks of lust as a shameful sin,
Says it's a highway to hell that beckons a man.
Calls it a crime that deserves punishment,
So he vowed to be clean and has kept his commitment.
He then speaks of the dignity he shows to all of his servants,
Everyone is created equally and each of them deserve it.
He says he hasn't trusted in money or gold,
Finding his security in anything he's owned.
He hasn't worshiped idols or denied the God of heaven,
He's never cursed anyone or rejoiced when their lives were threatened.
He has faithfully come to the aid of others,
Time and again taking care of sisters and brothers.
He's opened his door to strangers alike,
And has been a safe haven when disasters strike.
Now Job is the one who needs reassurance,
That Someone is listening and taking note of his grievance.

He knows that there's another that continues to blame and shame him,
But what he doesn't know is it's the Accuser of the Brethren.
That sneaky old snake that appeared in the Garden,
Has come before God and made this bargain.
It's been him all along at work in this story,
Stripping life and hope from Job, but God will get the glory.
It's all just been a momentary test,
Remember again that it was God who did suggest–
That He allowed Satan to do his evil deeds,
Because He was certain that Job would stay true to the Almighty.
So let's be sure to understand,
That God always stays faithful to His divine plan.
In this life, we will all have tests and trials,
And sometimes they'll catch us by surprise.
But nothing is hidden or takes God off-guard,
He can use anything to purify our hearts.
Even a serpent, a snake, a fallen angel...
God can bring good from what the enemy means for evil.
So we must always trust in His ways,
Remember He's the Potter and we are the clay.
He knows best and we can be sure,
His heart is kind and His motives are pure.

Don't Be Wise in Your Own Eyes (Job 32-34):

In this part of the conversation, we meet someone new.
He's young and he's angry, and his name is Elihu.
He tells the older men that he's waited his turn,
Listening to their words, his indignation began to burn.
He expected to hear wisdom come from their mouths,
But said their replies were pathetic so he had to speak out.
He corrected Job first since he refused to confess,
Before Almighty God his obvious sinfulness.
He tells Job and the others about the Spirit within,
That gives intelligence and wisdom but says it has eluded them.
They haven't represented God accurately,
He will give them true wisdom without flattery.
He says his words are pent up and must be released,
In sincerity and truth, he will now speak.
He rebukes Job for calling God unfair,
Says He works in many ways to show His loving care.
The Lord speaks to people again and again,
But they don't recognize His voice or turn to Him.
He comes in visions and dreams of the night,
Bringing warnings and terror to strip them of pride.
Sometimes, yes, there is discipline;
The body gets sick under the weight of sin.
This isn't always the way that it works,
We do live in this world under the curse.

And God often chooses to rescue us from death,
Revive us with life and continue to give us breath.
Elihu says it's due to faithful intercession,
That God reverses course and brings this resurrection.
He says that the person rescued from the grave,
Should give God all the glory and repent of his ways.
He continues his rebuke of Job,
Says his punishment was deserved for the words against God he spoke.
He accuses Job of being arrogant,
Instead of admitting fault, he continues to claim he's innocent.
He will now come to the Lord's defense,
And present arguments for His Creator's righteousness.
He tells them the Almighty doesn't sin like us,
He treats all as they deserve and will not twist justice.
That He is the Maker of heaven and earth,
And when He removes His breath of life we each return to the dirt.
He reminds them God is always watching everything we do;
And He's the one who decides when our time here is through.
He sets up kings and tears down nations,
He works in various ways to get our attention.
He has a heart for the poor and needy,
And when judgment is due, it is fair and speedy.
Elihu then says that people just need to admit
They have sinned against God and their hearts have been wicked.
He would show them mercy if they would just come clean,
Repent of their ways and know that they are seen.
Much of what was said here, again, is correct,
We must not add rebellion to our sin, showing God disrespect.
But this young man showed his own arrogance,
Claiming to have knowledge and fully understand.
He tells Job and his friends that not one of them were wise,
But then he professes to be (in his own eyes).

So much to learn from this continued interaction,
We should each check our own hearts for any infraction.
As we've seen all along in this story of wisdom,
None of us know it all and our perspective is limited.
God reveals Himself through creation and more,
And there is coming a Day that He'll settle the score.
But He is long-suffering, His patience unending,
Showing mercy and love and for mankind, always defending.
Giving us grace upon grace, without reservation,
Fully aware of our lack and desperation.
He comes to our aid again and again,
And through the blood of Jesus, takes away our sin.
We should each come in humility,
And bow before the Lord Almighty.

God Reveals His Power in Every Hour (Job 35-37):

Here we hear the end of Elihu's speech;
This final admonishment before the Lord speaks.
He continues to talk to Job about righteousness,
Responding to his previous claims that all of it is useless.
Elihu begins to introduce the men to the Almighty;
Says people's sinfulness or righteousness only affects humanity.
That it makes no difference to God if we walk in wickedness,
We don't add to or take away from Him with any of our goodness.
We benefit each other when our deeds are done in love,
When we emulate our Creator in the heavenlies above.
He speaks of the oppressed and how God hears their cries,
But says He doesn't answer them because of their pride.
He wonders why they don't seek for Him,
When He is the only One Who can help them.
He attributes to the Lord songs in the night,
Have you ever heard them singing in your mind?
I do sometimes and it's the neatest thing,
Waking up to a song about the Lord playing.
He says this is the God Who's always listening,
And that He also speaks to us, with both shouts and whispering.
That He is concerned with injustice and wickedness,
For Job to stop being foolish and speaking such nonsense.
He then boasts again of his great knowledge,
Says He will defend God and reveal to them His image.

God is mighty in power and understanding,
He despises no one and His love is everlasting.
He brings justice on those who are afflicted,
He always watches over the innocent.
They will rule and reign and He will exalt them,
This is the reward for faithfully walking with Him.
If they get caught in the snare of sin,
He will work in different ways to get their attention.
He shows them when they're living in pride,
And when they repent, He blesses their lives.
But if they refuse to heed His correction,
Their life takes a turn in the wrong direction.
Those who are godless are full of resentment,
They reject surrender in spite of their punishment.
They don't want to cry out to the Lord,
So they continue on in the ways of the world.
Their lives are immoral, full of wasted days,
Not realizing God was trying to lead them away.
Away from danger and the penalty of sin,
But in His lovingkindness, He forces no one to come in.
He always acts with great dignity,
If we want to reject Him, He allows us to stay at enmity.
What is true love if there is no choice?
He gives His call to all but we must respond to His voice.
He tells Job that God is setting his table,
Pulling him from danger and giving him the best that is available.
That he needs to stop being so obsessed,
With whether or not He will judge the godless.
He says not to worry, they will have their day;
God won't continue to let them go in the evil way.
But he warns Job to worry about himself,
Says not to be bribed into sin or lured away by wealth.

To be on guard and turn away from sin,
That God will save his life and has sent this suffering for a reason.
He is all-powerful and there is none like Him.
He is greater than we can even fathom.
No one can accuse Him of doing any wrong,
Instead we should sing of His glory with songs.
He deserves all of our awe and praise,
There is no beginning or end to His days.
He works in His creation mightily,
Turning vapor into rain and striking the earth with lightning.
He forms the clouds and they move through the sky,
He bellows forth His beckonings through thunder in the night.
God gives glimpses of Himself in flashes and booms,
Yet in His grandeur, He still takes notice of me and you!
He fills each of our lives with many good things,
Provision, purpose, and innumerable blessings.
Elihu reflected on all this truth about the Almighty,
Said it made his heart pound and he came to Him with trembling.
If each of us would listen carefully,
With His thunderous voice, He reveals His majesty.
He strikes with glory in every direction,
We can't even grasp His power and perfection.
He tells the sky when to bring snow,
And people stop their work to marvel at the show.
He directs the rain and even the wind,
The animals take cover and then go out again.
God brings the cold and causes it to freeze,
On the expanse of the waters and with the breath He breathes.
He works in all these ways to provide for people,
Showing grace and mercy to both the good and the evil.
Elihu tells Job to consider the Lord's miracles-
He works to craft everything with such precision and skill.

He asks if he is able to work in such ways,
And says if so, to teach all of them what to say.
That none of humanity is able to argue
With the God of creation and all of His statutes.
He is the One Who makes all the laws,
And His glory should make us each stand in awe.
His beauty and splendor is truly something to behold,
The sun, moon, and stars rejoice and His radiance is extolled.
This young man says that we should all be destroyed,
But that's not how God works and it's not the plan that He's employed.
Everyone with wisdom will show Him reverence,
And accept His invitation to come into His presence.
I marvel with Elihu at the descriptions that he gave,
Of God's wondrous power and His limitless grace.
To think that with a word, He set everything into motion,
And with each day that passes, He's restoring what we've broken.
I stand so amazed that I have a hard time finding words,
To adequately describe all God's goodness I've observed.
But all of what we've heard so far about the Lord
Is just a foretaste of the One Who's about to speak from the storm.

Remember God is Over All & We Are So Small (Job 38-39):

This is the day we've been waiting for,
The One Who does the speaking now is the Lord.
He comes to Job from the whirlwind,
In power and might and with many questions.
Can you even imagine a storm cloud touching down,
And thundering from it, the Almighty asking for an account?
He tells Job to brace himself like a man,
Because He has some questions and an answer He demands.
He said that Job's spoken in such ignorance,
Who is he to question things he doesn't understand?
God asks where he was when He laid the earth's foundations,
Magnificently revealing His hand in all creation.
He determined the dimensions of all the earth contains,
Laid the cornerstone as the morning stars sang.
He said this made the angels praise Him joyfully with shouts,
But as far as He knows, at this time, Job was nowhere to be found.
He tells him of the roaring seas - how He keeps the waters in place,
That it is the Almighty Who gives permission to the waves.
They can't reach any farther than He says they can,
And morning arises in the east at the word of His command.
He causes day to come and bring an end to the night,
Exposing all the wickedness and violence to the light.
He speaks of the many colors the sunlight puts in motion,
And asks Job again if he knows the vastness of the ocean.

Says to answer Him if he is aware of the gates of death,
And to tell Him of their location since he's so sure of the earth's great depth.
He confronts Job in his arrogance,
Saying He can see he's so experienced.
He was surely there at the time God created,
All that exists and his input was appreciated.
This seems like sarcasm from God on high,
He doesn't need any of our opinions or advice.
He speaks next about what He's reserved,
He has storehouses of snow and hail being preserved.
He says that these are weapons for the Day of trouble,
I imagine that a battle with the Lord would leave the earth in rubble.
God tells Job that He also brings the rain,
And this produces food for people to be sustained.
He has a plan and a cycle for life,
The rain, the dew, the frost, and the ice.
It all comes from Him and nourishes the land,
He's so methodical and thoughtful in every work of His hands.
He next asks Job if he can guide the constellations,
Or use the universe's laws to give earth her regulations.
He questions if he has the power to shout,
And bring down rain out of the clouds.
Of course he can't and neither can we,
We should bow before our Maker in humility.
He asks Job if he can send the lightning
Pointing out exactly where each bolt should be striking.
He says that He is the only One Who knows,
How many clouds are in the sky and where each of them goes.
He's also the One Who brings the relief of rain,
When the ground is dried up and the soil becomes clay.
Job hasn't once provided food for the lions,

Or brought nourishment when young ravens were crying.
This is all done by the God Who's set apart,
The One Who gives intuition to man's wanting heart.
He also fills our minds with such great wisdom,
Gives instinct and understanding, and causes us to listen.
The Lord continues probing Job,
Speaking next of deer and goats.
Asking if he knows when and how they give birth,
That once the young grows up and leaves, it never returns.
He tells of how the wild donkey and oxen are free,
Dependent on no one and this is the way He wants it to be.
He has given these animals a home,
On all of the earth, they may freely roam.
He talks about the unmatched speed of the ostrich,
She has instincts for survival but is lacking in knowledge.
He compares her to the horse, in all his majesty,
With its flowing mane, great strength, and ability.
Says it's unafraid of going out to war,
It rejoices in its power and goes forth with a terrifying snort.
The horse doesn't fear when the day of battle comes,
He charges swiftly onward and makes his presence known.
God asks Job if it's due to his wisdom,
That the hawk and the eagle glide in such precision,
And how they hunt for prey, if that is his doing;
Watching with their eyes, patiently pursuing.
We're at the end of this portion, but God's not done yet.
We'll pick up with Job's brief reply of regret.
Then the Almighty will speak again
And tell Job about the power of Leviathan.
I believe He is using this comparison
To illustrate to him just how mighty He is in all of creation.
But I won't get ahead of myself,

I'll meet you in the next chapter for the part I like best.

The End of Job's Story, All For God's Glory (Job 40-42):

This is our last encounter from the Book of Job,
God speaks again, continuing to probe.
He confronts Job for arguing with Him,
Asks if he has all the answers or just more criticism.
Job responds to God appropriately,
Vows to be silent as he's said too much already.
The Lord then comes from the whirlwind again,
With some more questions and wants answers for them.
He tells him the second time to brace himself as a man,
Who is he to claim His justice doesn't stand?
God asks why he discredits and condemns Him,
Is he trying to prove he is right before his friends?
The Lord asks Job if he's as strong as He is,
If so, speak out in a thunderous voice like His.
Tells him to put on majesty and honor,
Clothe himself in glory and splendor.
Says to send down all of his fury,
To play both the judge and the jury.
Bring vengeance on all of the wicked,
Imprison them in the world of the dead.
He tells Job that if he is able to pull this off,
Even He would praise him for his strength like Behemoth.
He said that surely he could save himself,
If he knows how to run the earth so well.

God mentions the physique of this mighty creature,
Describing in detail all of its features.
He points to it as an example of His great handiwork.
And reminds Job that both it and he were made by the Lord.
He provides for both, giving all that they need;
And no one can threaten their existence but He.
God then begins to speak about Leviathan,
Another majestic work of His hands.
This creature sounds to me like a dinosaur,
There are debates about this, so we don't know for sure.
Whatever it was, it was a force to be reckoned with;
God said that it had such enormous strength.
No one on earth could be its master,
And they would be sorry if they tried to be his captor.
In the middle of giving this beast's description,
The Almighty posed a poignant question.
He asked Job who had ever given Him anything He needed to repay,
Everything under heaven is His, all the earth contains.
He doesn't need anyone's permission,
And He is the ultimate in authority and position.
He then resumes describing this creature,
Saying that down here, none is his equal.
It seems to me to be a parallel
To the way that He describes Himself.
He speaks of what comes from his nose and his mouth,
Lightning, smoke, and fiery flames flash out.
In other books and places in Scripture,
This is the way that the Lord is pictured.
So I believe He is making the connection,
He is unmatched in power and perfection.
He says Leviathan can't be conquered,
That he is fearless and proud, deserving to be honored.

After all that God says about this king of beasts,
He now gives Job another chance to speak.
So he comes back with this reply:
"You asked who questioned You and it was I...
I spoke of things too lofty for me,
I'd only heard of You before, but now I've seen."
Job confessed to the Lord that he was wrong,
That he should have just kept quiet all along.
He now sits in ashes and dust,
Takes back all that he said and shows repentance.
This is the best thing we can all do-
Humble ourselves and repent when we need to.
After God finished speaking to Job,
He chastised his friends for the words that they spoke.
He told them He was angry at the things they had said,
They didn't speak accurately of Him as Job had.
So the only way they could be made clean
Was to go to Job with a burnt offering.
He told them that Job would then pray to Him,
On their behalf and He'd forgive their sin.
He said a second time that they hadn't spoken truthfully,
The way His servant Job had, but He would show them mercy.
So the friends brought their offering as the Lord had commanded,
Then Job prayed for each of them and forgiveness was granted.
When his prayer of faith arose to the Lord,
All that Job had lost was kindly restored.
And God didn't just give him the same as before,
He blessed him abundantly with even more!
All his friends and family returned,
To console Job and bring him comfort.
They knew the Lord had brought these trials,
So they came to feast and be reconciled.

God was good to His servant Job,
He gave back his possessions but most importantly, his hope.
He blessed him with seven sons and three daughters,
A true story of redemption that only God could author.
The writer of this book then gives us some details;
Describing his daughters and saying they were in Job's will.
In those days, this wasn't usual practice,
Only a man's sons were left an inheritance.
I suspect the reason that this is included,
Is so we can see that from God's grace, no one is excluded.
Job was so grateful to be back in His favor,
That from his faith, he would never waver.
The Lord did give him a long, full life.
He lived 140 more years and saw four generations before he died.
So the end of his story, as I said earlier on,
Is one of tragedy turned to hope as the curtain is drawn.
I pray that I've done justice to tell of this account,
And highlight everything that the Lord wanted me to recount.
I have enjoyed traveling with you through Job,
And I'll leave you now with this: There is always hope.

Bonus: Praying Through Job
Job 1-5:

Heavenly Father,

Glory to Your mighty name!!! We don't see things as You see them. We don't see what or who is around You and what they are saying or doing. We don't see our Accuser or hear the things he says about us in Your presence. But may You be so sure of our character (in Christ) that You would come to our defense and even SUGGEST us to him, that we would be sifted in a way that would purify us and make us more like Your Son. We know that You work all things together for our good, and that whether tests in our lives come directly from Your hands or You use and allow him to sift us as wheat...either way, may we trust Your plan. May we trust Your heart. May we heed Your correction and come under the shelter of Your mighty wings. May we repent where repentance is needed, and praise be to You for Your kindness that leads us here. And may we say with Job and with full assurance, "The Lord gives and the Lord takes away....blessed be the Name of the Lord." Amen and amen.

Job 6-9:

Heavenly Father,

How often do we wrestle in our pain and trials just like Job? We don't understand all that is going on behind the scenes. Job did not know that You were allowing this time of testing BECAUSE You were so sure of his integrity and faithfulness. All he could see were his circumstances. So many times, this is the way it is for us too. Also, in this exchange, we see friends who thought they knew all the answers–they knew You, they knew the reasons You brought all of this pain to Job, and they apparently knew something that even Job wasn't aware of–sin in his own heart. We can be so quick to judge others and point fingers, even insist things about Who You are and why You do certain things. Forgive us, Father, and teach us to keep our mouths shut more often. Teach us to just sit with our friends and family when they are suffering. Help us learn the worshipful act of silence. Tear down our pride, that we would not seek to be heard so often, but rather to hear Your still small voice and hear others. To seek to understand and show compassion, empathy, and love. The way that You do. Give us the desire to intercede in prayer on their behalf, rather than interject and impose our own thoughts and opinions on them. I thank You for sending the Mediator that Job pleaded for...that Jesus has come so we may have life abundant in You. Praise be to Your holy and mighty name. Teach us to be like Jesus our Lord. In His name we pray, amen.

Job 10-13:

Our sweet, sweet all-knowing Father,

We love You. We lift Your name on high, the Name above all names. You alone are worthy. King of kings and Lord of lords. May we come before Your throne now to find Your mercy and grace. Only a God so full of love and compassion would allow us entry to His throne room and come beside us in our pain and sorrows. We thank You that even when we don't have all the answers, we can entrust ourselves and our lives to Your control, knowing that You are at work in all things and at all times. May our trust in You just continue to grow and multiply, that when we are faced with the "why's" of life, we quickly lay them down in surrender, knowing in our hearts that You know best and if you see fit for us to experience a trial or testing, we say, "Yes, Lord," bring it. Because we know that with it, we get all of Your loving guidance, gentle correction, and comforting peace. And we come out on the other side refined and restored, and that You get the glory for the transformation. Amen and amen, in Jesus' name.

Job 14-16:

Dear Lord Almighty,

Help us have a proper view of Who You are and how You work in creation and all around us, especially in Your redemptive plan of salvation. May we see ourselves for who we really are and may it humble us and move us to fix our eyes on You, the Author and Finisher of our faith. Just as Job wrestled with his human emotions and his limited understanding of Your ways, so do we. I pray that we receive Your abundant mercy and grace and that we seek to pour it out on others around us. Make us a vessel fit for Your Kingdom work, the good works You have already prepared for us to walk in long before the foundations of the world. Your plan has always been in place and we are a part of it. Hallelujah, in Jesus' name! Amen.

Job 17-20:

Father in Heaven,

Lord, it is an honor to come before You as a willing, broken vessel. Allow Your words to continue to flow through me each morning, as I seek to honor You with all of who I am. I pray for every person who may ever read or hear these words, that somehow You would use them to penetrate their mind and heart. Maybe they have never understood how much You love them or how many times You have called them to Yourself...how many invitations You have given them to receive Your forgiveness and grace that they have never fully surrendered to and received. Please open their hearts and minds today to grasp this truth—that our Redeemer lives—and that in order to see Him and be united with Him, they must put all of their faith, hope, and trust in You. It is not hard to get to know You...You are all around us and we see Your hand in everything that's been made. You are beautiful to behold and it makes my soul sing. Your heart is for us and it is always good. No matter our circumstances, may we stand on the truth of Your Word, the free and undeserved gift of salvation through Your Son, and the gentleness of Your sweet, abiding Spirit. Envelop each person in Your great care today, I pray. In Jesus' name, amen.

Job 21-23:

Dear Lord Jesus,

We love You and thank You for Your goodness, kindness, and grace, which is extended to every single one of us, every single day. None of us deserve anything but death and hell, but praise be to Your holy name–this is NOT what we get! You give us YOURSELF, having sacrificed Your very life for ours. Thank You for Your forgiveness and gift of everlasting life. You also lavish on us Your many, many blessings. May our hearts sing Your praise today and every day. In Jesus' name, amen.

Job 24-28:

Heavenly Father,

We love to see Your hand in creation. This story of Job, which can seem at times so tragic and hopeless, is also a great testament to Your work in our world and the intimacy of how You orchestrate things in each of our lives. May we not miss the splendor of Your glory by having a limited view of ourselves and our circumstances. May we behold You in all of Your greatness. From Your guiding and loving hand, the whole earth and all that it contains was created. Each and every person, plant, animal, EVERYTHING!!!! And not only do You create, but You sustain us with life and breath every single day until Your appointed time to return us each to the dirt. You spoke a Word and everything came into being. Then You breathed the breath of life into mankind. WOW...and if that wasn't enough, You loved this world that You made SO MUCH that You sacrificed Your only Son so that we may have the opportunity to come to You in repentance over our rebellion and rejection and be made righteous, that we may live with You for all of eternity. How wonderful You are!!!!! I pray today that in the mighty name of Jesus, every knee will bow NOW and surrender all to You, that they may walk in the newness of life today...so that they will live with You forever. Amen.

Job 29-31:

Almighty God, Maker of heaven and earth,
You put the stars in the heavens and You know them by name. You knitted each of us in our mother's womb and You know us by name. You are so wonderful to allow us entry into this world and even more-so, entry into eternal life through Your Son. Reading Your Word just makes our hearts long for that day when we can be with You for all of forever. The awesome thing is, though, that You allow us entry NOW into Your throne-room...that we can come boldly before Your throne through Jesus and speak to You directly. You are not some far-off deity...You are a loving, caring, good, good Father Who grants us access anywhere at any time and You actually long to hear from us, to interact with us, to walk and talk with us. To shower Your love and mercy upon us and envelop us in Your great care. How magnificent You are. I pray that You wrap Your loving arms around any person reading this prayer today...that they would understand with all the saints, the length and breadth and height and depths of Your great love toward them, which You have shown all the world in the priceless gift of Your Son. May each person experience Your love in a new and deep way today and be drawn into Yourself by the power of the Holy Spirit and the truth of Your Word. In Jesus' name, amen.

Job 32-34:

Father God,

We come to You today, bowing our knees in humility. Thank You for creating us all. Thank You for life and breath and that in You, we move and have our being. Thank You for the way You work in our life and give us chance after chance to turn from our wicked ways and turn to You. Thank You for Your Word, that we can learn what wickedness is, and for Your Spirit, which empowers us to walk in a manner worthy of our high calling as sons and daughters. A real son or daughter loves their parent with all their heart, soul, mind, and strength and willingly comes up under submission to the parent. This is what You desire and require of us and is a good first step for any of us to see if we are truly Your child. Are You first in our life and heart? Do we bow the knee and not put anything or any person above Your rightful place in authority over us? May we each examine ourselves today in Your presence and if we find ourselves wanting, You offer us repentance...anytime, anywhere. And we praise You for Your goodness and grace. We love You, Lord. In Jesus' name, amen.

Job 35-37:

Lord,
We lift Your name on high. We come into Your courts with praise and thanksgiving and today, we simply want to sit in silence and ponder on Your power. Let's do that now. In Jesus' name, amen.

Job 38-39:

Father in Heaven,

You are so mighty, so wonderful, so deserving of all our praise and more. We love You and we bow humbly in submission before Your throne of grace. Thank You for being unlike us, supreme and perfect in all You do. Who are we to question You? We lay all of who we are at Your feet and ask You to simply guide and correct us when we get too big for our britches. We need You and we love You. You are the Potter and we are the clay. Mold us today and every day, in Jesus' name. Amen.

Job 40-42:

Dear Lord,

We come to You today and evaluate ourselves. Who of us has any room to question or doubt Your goodness, mercy, grace...Your character, Your will, Your plan? I pray that if we have had a haughty or know-it-all spirit about us, that we would sit in repentance before You and confess that we know nothing, as Job did. It's so easy for us to allow our environment to shape our view of You rather than standing on Who we know You to be and seeing our circumstances through the lens of Your goodness and grace. Even when bad things happen in our lives, we should not attribute these things to You. We know that we have an enemy of our souls who accuses us day and night in Your courts and that Jesus defends those of us who are His!! Anything that he wants to bring upon us though, must be granted Your permission, and if you allow or will testing in our life, it is ultimately for our good—to make us more like Christ, Your Son. The ultimate goal. We are refined and purified as we go THROUGH the fire and there is no way around it. So, I pray that You would grant each person who reads this today an understanding of suffering...a heart that is soft and ready to receive the love and peace that only You can provide, one that passes all understanding. And I pray that these hard times would serve to only draw us closer to Yourself, the One Who can heal all wounds and Who is a loving Father, always at work in and through the creation He made. Thank You for the book of Job and the lessons we learn from this tragic tale turned to hope. May we say with Job, "The Lord gives and the Lord takes away, blessed be the name of the Lord." I pray I brought honor to Your name through the poems Your

Spirit spoke through me, Lord, and that someone may understand this story in a new way today. It's in the precious name of Christ my King I pray, amen.

Don't miss out!

Visit the website below and you can sign up to receive emails whenever Angela Williams publishes a new book. There's no charge and no obligation.

https://books2read.com/r/B-A-TWXAB-KQGPC

BOOKS 2 READ

Connecting independent readers to independent writers.

Did you love *The Poetry Project: Job*? Then you should read *The Poetry Project: Genesis*[1] by Angela Williams!

[2]

Do you enjoy poetry? Would you love to hear some of the harder-to-read portions of God's Word retold in rhythmic form? This is just what I've set out to do so that all of Scripture comes alive and is easy to understand and enjoy. Some people tend to think the God of the Old Testament is angry compared to Jesus in the New Testament, but it is my mission to show you that He is the same God - yesterday, today, and forever. And His love knows no bounds. I firmly believe that even if you do not love poetry or have belong to the Christian faith, you will still enjoy this book! This is part of a series, so be sure to pick up my other "The Poetry Project" books as well!

---

1. https://books2read.com/u/bW6vw7

2. https://books2read.com/u/bW6vw7

Read more at https://angelawilliams1006.wixsite.com/ unapologeticallyme.

Also by Angela Williams

The Poetry Project
The Poetry Project: Genesis
The Poetry Project: Job

Watch for more at https://angelawilliams1006.wixsite.com/
unapologeticallyme.

About the Author

I am a southern girl, born and raised in a small Southeast Texas town. I love hard and big and am unapologetically a coffee drinking, Jesus loving "Mamaw!" I enjoy writing (mostly poetry), spending time with the Lord and my family, and my soul comes alive out in God's beautiful creation. It is my mission to reach the world with the love of Christ in whatever capacity He allows.

Read more at https://angelawilliams1006.wixsite.com/unapologeticallyme.

www.ingramcontent.com/pod-product-compliance
Lightning Source LLC
Chambersburg PA
CBHW021321160726
47994CB00004B/1547